PIANO TIME 3

new edition

Pauline Hall

MUSIC DEPARTMENT

OXFORD
UNIVERSITY PRESS

Starting out

◆ Before you start this book, let's check up on a few important things.

Notes at the edges

◆ Are you confident about the **high** and **low** notes in each hand?

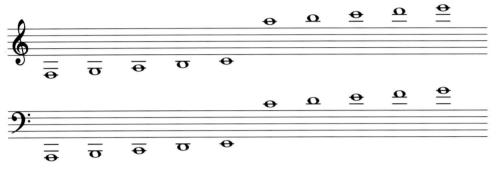

Time signatures

◆ Are you sure about the time signatures at the start of pieces?

$\frac{4}{4}$ means four crotchets (or quarter-notes) in a bar; sometimes shown as **C**

$\frac{2}{4}$ means two crotchets (or quarter-notes) in a bar

$\frac{6}{8}$ means six quavers (or eighth-notes) in a bar

$\frac{3}{2}$ means three minims (or half-notes) in a bar

$\frac{3}{8}$ means three quavers (or eighth-notes) in a bar

Signs

◆ Can you remember these signs which you learnt in *Piano Time 2*?

♩ (tenuto)	tenuto; give the note a little extra **accent**
8va - - - ⌐	this sign means play the notes an **octave higher**
8va bassa	this sign means play the notes an **octave lower**
𝄢. ✳	signs to press and release the right (sustaining) pedal

Musical words

◆ Do you remember what these words mean?

Moderato	at a moderate speed
Rallentando	becoming gradually slower; sometimes shortened to **rall.**
legato	smoothly
diminuendo	getting quieter; also written as *dim.*
crescendo	getting louder; also written as *cresc.*
Da Capo	go back to the beginning (of a piece); sometimes written **D.C.**
Fine	the end

Helpful hints for good practice

You can't be a good athlete or swimmer without a lot of practice, and it's the same with playing the piano. But to be good, the practice needs to be the right kind. Here are a few helpful hints for practice that will improve your playing.

When and how

- Aim for a **short practice every day**. This is much better than leaving it for several days or a long frantic practice just before your lesson!
- **Don't neglect your scales**. They will reward you if you practise them regularly.
- Think of practice like sports training. Warm up with some scales or exercises, then do some work on your pieces, and finish (warm down) by playing a favourite piece you've learnt before.
- Approach your practice session ready to learn. Think about what you're doing and concentrate as you play.

Practising your pieces

- Start with each hand **separately** when learning a new piece, and count steadily.
- Practise **slowly**. You can only get a quick piece right with slow practice.
- Places where you make mistakes need special practice. Keep playing these through until they feel secure. It's better to concentrate on the tricky bits than always play a piece through from start to finish.
- Learn your **fingering**. Always use the same fingering so that your fingers know where to go.
- Check your **hand position,** as this is very important. Your fingers should be nicely curved and on their tips—no flat fingers and drooping wrists (and *no* clicking finger-nails!).
- When you can play a piece through without any mistakes, why not get someone to listen to you play it?

Enjoy your practice, and remember: **Practice Makes Perfect.**

Semiquavers

◆ A **semiquaver** (or sixteenth-note) looks like a quaver with two tails: ♪

◆ Semiquavers are usually grouped together in fours ♬♬ or in twos ♬

◆ 'Semi' means 'half', so a semiquaver is worth half a quaver:

Tortoise and hare

Pauline Hall

Steady semiquaver study

Pauline Hall

4

Semiquaver work-page

Rhythm words

◆ All words have a natural rhythm.

◆ Say and clap these words: **Caterpillar**
Centipede
Spider
Snail

◆ Can you write them as notes? Each word must be worth one crotchet ♩

'Butterfly' is given as an example.

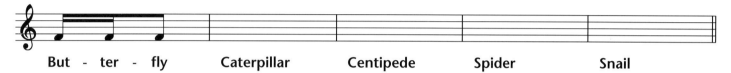

| But – ter – fly | Caterpillar | Centipede | Spider | Snail |

Rhythmic rhyme

◆ Now write the rhythm of the rhyme below. Each bar must be worth two crotchets ♩ ♩

Kookaburra sits on the   old   gum   tree,   Merry, merry king of the   bush   is   he.

Rhythm box

◆ A rhythm for each of these lines is scattered around the page. Choose the right one and write it in the correct box.

Each box is worth one crotchet ♩

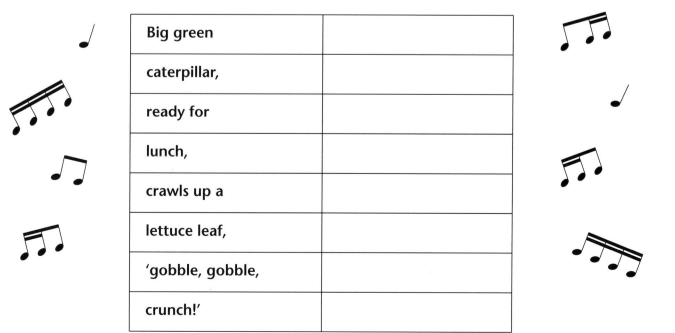

Big green	
caterpillar,	
ready for	
lunch,	
crawls up a	
lettuce leaf,	
'gobble, gobble,	
crunch!'	

English dance

Allegretto

James Hook (1746–1827)

Sailors' hornpipe

Very steadily

arr. by Pauline Hall

Keys

◆ You already know two keys that have sharps:

The key of **G** with **F♯**:

and the key of **D** with **F♯** and **C♯**:

◆ The next key (with a third sharp added) is the key of **A**, with **F♯**, **C♯**, and **G♯**:

◆ This is how the sharps are added to make new keys. Starting with **C** which has no sharps,

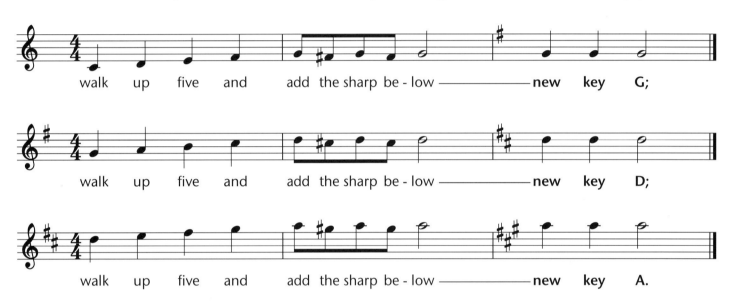

walk   up   five   and   add the sharp be-low —————— **new   key   G**;

walk   up   five   and   add the sharp be-low —————— **new   key   D**;

walk   up   five   and   add the sharp be-low —————— **new   key   A**.

◆ See if you can work out the next key which has four sharps, using the same pattern. Write the notes in the space provided.

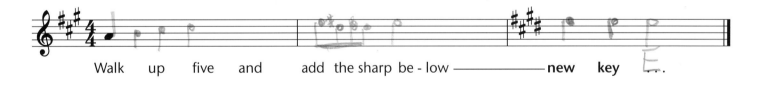

Walk   up   five   and   add the sharp be-low —————— **new   key**   E.

K·E·Y Q·U·I·Z

◆ Test your knowledge of the **sharp keys** with this quiz, which also gets you playing.

1. Here is a well-known tune from France. Check the key signature and then play it through.

Sur le pont d'Avignon

What key is it in? . . . .

2. Here's the start of the tune in a new key. **What key is it in now?** Can you finish playing the tune by ear?

Key: . . . .

What sharps did you play? . . . . and . . . .

3. Here's the start once more in another key. Write down the key and the sharp you played, and finish playing the tune by ear.

Key: . . . .

Sharp played: . . . .

4. Now try this folk tune from England. **What key is it in?** . . . .

Early one morning

5. Here's the opening in another key:

What key is it in? . . . .

What sharps did you play? . . . . and . . . . and . . . .

See if you can finish playing the tune by ear.

A major

◆ **A major** has three sharps—**F♯**, **C♯**, and **G♯**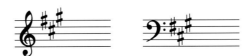

Scales

◆ The fingering in both hands is the same as for D major. Keep your fingers well forward on the keys to be ready for the sharps. Notice how nicely the black keys fit under your fingers!

One octave:

Two octaves:

Arpeggios

Right hand:

Left hand:

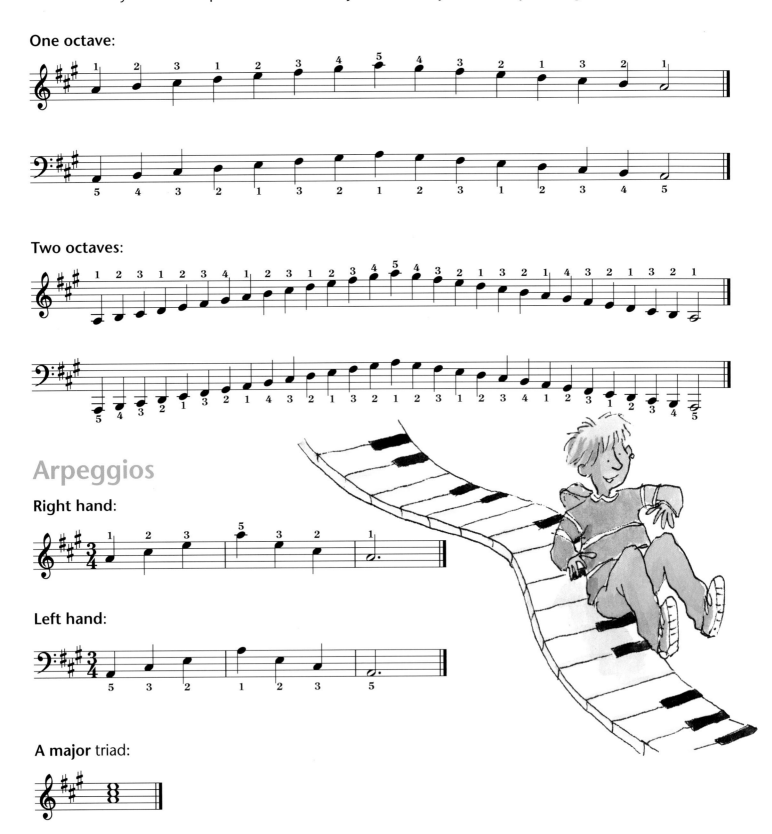

A major triad:

Dutch dance

◆ Your left hand stays over five notes and doesn't need to move. But look out for the left-hand accidental.

Gracefully

Pauline Hall

New semiquaver rhythm

- The next two pieces have a new **semiquaver rhythm**:

- Clap the first line of 'Donkey riding' as even quavers:

  were you ev - er   in Que-bec

- Now clap it with the dotted rhythm:

  were you ev - er   in Que-bec

- The second time the first note is longer and the semiquaver is tucked in at the end.

Donkey riding

Briskly

English sea song
arr. Pauline Hall

mf

Were you ev - er | in Que-bec, | stow-ing tim - ber

on the deck, | Where there's a king with a | gold-en crown | rid-ing on a | don - key?

f

Hey! Ho! a - way we go, | don - key rid - ing, | don - key rid - ing;

Hey!__ Ho! a - way we go, | rid - ing on a | don - key.

Country gardens

◆ This well-known piece is full of the rhythm: ♪. ♪

How many can you spot?

English Morris tune
arr. Pauline Hall

Moderato

Alberti bass

◆ On the piano you can use chords in the left hand to accompany a tune:

◆ Or you can break up these chords, rearranging the notes into a broken chord pattern, like this:

◆ This type of pattern is known as an **Alberti bass**. It was named after an Italian composer, Domenico Alberti, who lived in the 18th century and who used it in many of his keyboard pieces. Lots of other composers used it too.

◆ The secret of playing pieces with Alberti basses is to keep the left hand very quiet so that the tune in the right hand can be clearly heard.

Signore Alberti's gavotte

◆ Try playing an Alberti bass in this little piece.

Gracefully

Pauline Hall

Country gardens

◆ This well-known piece is full of the rhythm: ♩. ♪

How many can you spot?

English Morris tune
arr. Pauline Hall

Alberti bass

◆ On the piano you can use chords in the left hand to accompany a tune:

◆ Or you can break up these chords, rearranging the notes into a broken chord pattern, like this:

◆ This type of pattern is known as an **Alberti bass**. It was named after an Italian composer, Domenico Alberti, who lived in the 18th century and who used it in many of his keyboard pieces. Lots of other composers used it too.

◆ The secret of playing pieces with Alberti basses is to keep the left hand very quiet so that the tune in the right hand can be clearly heard.

Signore Alberti's gavotte

◆ Try playing an Alberti bass in this little piece.

Gracefully

Pauline Hall

Andante cantabile

◆ Here's another piece with an Alberti bass. **'Cantabile'** means to play in a 'singing' style, so make your right hand 'sing' the tune.

Roman Hoffstetter (1742–1815)*
arr. Pauline Hall

* This piece was formerly attributed to Joseph Haydn.

B♭ major

◆ **B♭ major** has two flats—B♭ and E♭

Scales

◆ The fingering in both hands is different from any other scale you've learnt so far, because the first note (B♭) is a black key. Here is the two-octave scale in both hands:

Right hand:

◆ **Golden rule:** 4th finger on all **B♭s** (except the first and last)
                 3rd finger on all **E♭s**

Left hand:

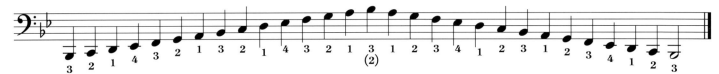

◆ **Golden rule:** 3rd finger on all **B♭s**
                 4th finger on all **E♭s**

◆ Practise these **slowly** until you feel you know them.

Arpeggios

◆ The arpeggio fingering is also different, again to avoid a thumb on the black key.

Right hand:

Left hand:

B♭ major triad:

◆ **Helpful hint:** in all scales which have black keys in them, including B♭ major, keep your fingers well forward on the keys, so that the black keys are easy to reach and lie comfortably under your fingers.

Summer swing

◆ Try putting down the **sustaining pedal** for the last two bars.

Pauline Hall

A new rhythm in ⁶⁄₈ time

◆ You know that in ⁶⁄₈ there are six quavers in the bar, grouped in two sets of three:

◆ ♪♪♪ can be altered to make a new rhythm. If you make the first note longer (by adding a dot) and the next one shorter (by making it a semiquaver) to balance, you get the rhythm: ♩.♪♪

◆ Clap this lullaby and feel the lilt of this rhythm:

Rock - a-bye ba - by   on   the tree top.

Greensleeves

English folksong

Gently

mp

Skye boat song

◆ The 'lad that's born to be king' was Bonnie Prince Charlie, and this song tells of his escape from his enemies to the Scottish island of Skye in 1746.

Scottish ballad

Speed bon-nie boat   like a   bird on the wing,   'On-ward' the sail - ors   cry.

Car - ry the lad   that's   born   to be king,   O - ver the sea   to   Skye.

Fine

Loud the winds howl,   loud the waves roar,   Thun-der-claps rend   the   air.

Baf - fled our foes   stand by   the shore,   Fol - low they will   not   dare.

D.C. al Fine

19

Left-hand keep-fit

◆ This page will help keep your left hand fit and nimble.

Left-hand landmarks

◆ Three landmarks for quick route-finding:

Top line A

Ground floor G   **Dog in the middle**

Chord spotting

◆ Play this triad chord and notice its shape. Using the same fingering, play other chords with the same shape.

◆ Here is another chord of a different shape. Notice that there is only one key between the bottom two notes, and two keys between the top two. Play some more chords of the same shape, using the same fingers.

◆ Play this new chord shape and get the feel of it. Notice that you use your 2nd finger for the middle note. Play some more chords of this shape.

Invent your own basses

◆ First play these chords:

◆ Now try rearranging them in different ways.

Here they sound like a waltz:

and here they make a cowboy rhythm:

Triad trickster

Allegro

Pauline Hall

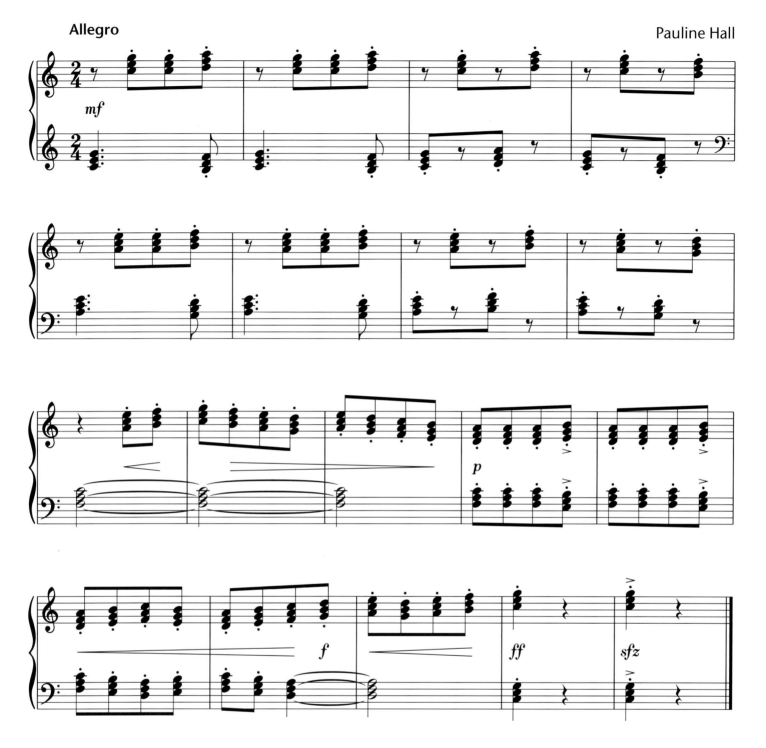

- ◆ Keep your hand in a triad-shape all through this piece, using fingers 1, 3, and 5 only. All the triads move by step, which means they are always next door to each other, moving up or down.

- ◆ When you can play it, try the trick! Cross your hands, and make your left hand play the right-hand part, and the right hand the left.
Easy? Well . . .

- ◆ In the last bar **sfz** is short for *sforzando*, meaning 'accented' or 'forced'.

Finger-twisters

◆ Tongue-twisters help loosen up the tongue (try saying 'She sells sea-shells on the sea-shore' quickly), and these finger-twisters will make your fingers nimble and strong. Important! If you want to be able to play these fast, you *must* practise them slowly.

◆ You don't have to play them all at once. Try some now, then later on in the book come back and play some more.

In and out

◆ Use the two-bar space to add your own finger-twisters. Use the notes C, D, E, F, and G only, in any order you like.

Out and in

◆ Left hand's turn. Add your own two bars at the end.

Hold on!

◆ Time for your right hand again. Keep the chords held down while the other fingers play.

◆ Now your left hand.

Two by two

◆ This one doesn't need to go too fast; the aim is to play the notes really evenly. Try it *legato* and then *staccato*. If you're feeling *very* strong, try with hands together.

Quick change

◆ Really crisp finger changes are needed with this finger-twister.

Climbing chords

◆ Aim for strong fingers climbing through the chords. When you've learnt the pattern, try starting on G and in other keys too.

Scales hands together, one octave

◆ The secret is to play these **very slowly**, until your fingers know where to go. The fingering *must* be right.

Scaling the cliff

◆ Here's an exercise to help. Imagine a scale is like a climb up and down a cliff. There are stopping places where you rest and think how you are going to go on.

◆ The 3rd finger notes are the stopping places. When you get to these, STOP . . . HAVE A THINK . . . and then GO ON YOUR WAY.

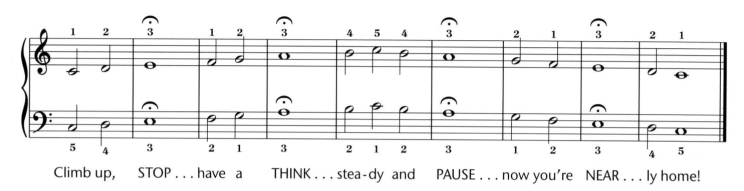

Climb up,   STOP . . . have a   THINK . . . stea-dy and   PAUSE . . . now you're   NEAR . . . ly home!

◆ Practise the climb a lot, and when you feel safe, try shortening the resting times. Your hands will soon become good climbers!

C major

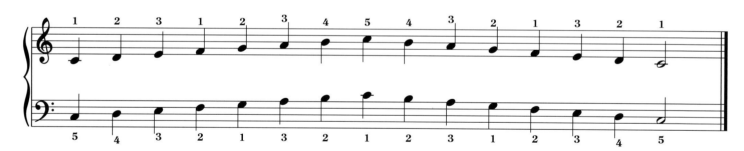

G major

24

P·I·A·N·O T·I·M·E

OXFORD

The award-winning Piano Time is a hugely successful series for all budding pianists, taking young pupils from their very first lesson up to around Grade 3 standard.

With a full range of carefully paced and attractive books — teaching and technique books, pieces and duets — Piano Time is an enjoyable way to teach and learn the piano.

‹ A breath of fresh air for teachers and pupils alike ›

Piano Journal

Young beginners

Tunes for Ten Fingers
An introductory book for young absolute
beginners

Fun for Ten Fingers
Pieces in five-finger position — a bridge between
Tunes for Ten Fingers and *More Tunes for Ten
Fingers*

More Tunes for Ten Fingers
Pieces following on from *Fun for Ten Fingers*,
with lots of songs, duets, puzzles, and games

Piano Time Carols
Really easy arrangements of
the most popular carols

Piano Time 1 (pre-Grade 1)

Piano Time 1
Starts at the very beginning,
with simple five-finger tunes
for hands separately and
together

Piano Time Pieces 1
Pieces in varied styles
practising the techniques and
keys used in *Piano Time 1*

Piano Time
Sightreading Book 1
Lots of short tunes in five-
finger position, mostly hands
separately, with helpful tips

Piano Time Sports
Book 1
Warm-up exercises and
short pieces to practise new
techniques; chords, hand-
crossing, scales

Piano Time Carols
Really easy arrangements of
the most popular carols

Duets with a
Difference
Imaginative duets in
popular styles with superb
illustrations and listening
games

Piano Time 2 (approx. Grade 1)

Piano Time 2
Builds on *Piano Time 1*, and
includes pieces using chords
and triads, arpeggios, scales,
and pedalling

Piano Time Pieces 2
Pieces in varied styles
practising the techniques an
keys used in *Piano Time 2*

Piano Time Sports
Book 1
Warm-up exercises and shor
pieces to practise new
techniques; chords, hand-
crossing, scales

Piano Time Sports
Book 2
Warm-up exercises and
short pieces to practise new
techniques; broken chords,
octaves, scales

Piano Time
Sightreading Book 2
Short exercises in five-
finger position, introducing
accidentals and hands-
together

Practice makes Perfe
Progressive technique
exercises with useful tips an
listening games

Piano Time Dance
NEW
Fun pieces in a dazzling arr
of dance styles

OXFORD

Piano Time Classics
Really easy graded arrangements of popular classical tunes

More Piano Time Classics
Really easy arrangements of favourite classical tunes that we all know and love

Piano Time Opera
Really simple arrangements of operatic masterpieces

Prehistoric Piano Time
An entertaining mix of dinosaur pieces, games, and puzzles

Piano Time Jazz Book 1
Accessible pieces in jazz and light-hearted styles using syncopation and cool harmonies

Spooky Piano Time
Repertoire pieces, puzzles, poems, and full-colour illustrations on supernatural themes

Mixed Doubles
20 classical, jazzy, and folk duets, with fun listening games

Piano Time Jazz Duets Book 1
Easy duets in jazzy and light styles from energetic boogie to moody blues

Piano Time 3

Piano Time 3
Introduces new keys, semi-quavers, triplets, and melodic minors, and practises scales with hands together

Piano Time Pieces 3
Enjoyable repertoire material practising the range of techniques and keys introduced in *Piano Time 3*

Piano Time Sightreading Book 3
Exercises using hands together and changes of position in varied time signatures and styles

Piano Time Sports Book 2
Warm-up exercises and short pieces to practise new techniques; broken chords, octaves, scales

Practice makes Perfect
Progressive technique exercises with useful tips, listening games; includes staccato, stretching, repeated notes, ornaments, hand-crossing

Piano Time Dance
NEW
Fun pieces in a dazzling array of dance styles

Piano Time Going Places
Varied pieces on the themes of travel and movement with illustrations by Korky Paul

Piano Time Jazz Book 2
Easy and stylish toe-tapping duets in jazzy and light-hearted styles

Mixed Doubles
20 classical, jazzy, and folk duets, with fun listening games

Piano Time Jazz Duets Book 2
Stylish duets for students around *Piano Time 3* standard; boogie-woogie, swing, gospel, blues

Teaching books

Duet books

Technique books

Repertoire books

Teaching books

Tunes for Ten Fingers
978-0-19-372738-0

Fun for Ten Fingers
978-0-19-372767-0

More Tunes for Ten Fingers
978-0-19-372739-7

Piano Time 1
978-0-19-372784-7

Piano Time 2
978-0-19-372786-1

Piano Time 3
978-0-19-372788-5

Technique books

Piano Time Sightreading
Book 1: 978-0-19-372768-7
Book 2: 978-0-19-372769-4
Book 3: 978-0-19-372770-0

Piano Time Sports
Book 1: 978-0-19-372773-1
Book 2: 978-0-19-372774-8

Practice makes Perfect
978-0-19-357025-2

Duet books

Duets with a Difference
978-0-19-372753-3

Mixed Doubles
978-0-19-372754-0

Piano Time Jazz Duets
Book 1: 978-0-19-335597-2
Book 2: 978-0-19-335598-9

Repertoire books

Piano Time Pieces 1
978-0-19-372785-4

Piano Time Pieces 2
978-0-19-372787-8

Piano Time Pieces 3
978-0-19-372789-2

Piano Time Carols
978-0-19-372737-3

Piano Time Classics
978-0-19-372736-6

More Piano Time Classics
978-0-19-372749-6

NEW
Piano Time Dance
978-0-19-337005-0

Piano Time Going Places
978-0-19-372730-4

Piano Time Jazz
Book 1: 978-0-19-372733-5
Book 2: 978-0-19-372734-2

Piano Time Opera
978-0-19-372762-5

Prehistoric Piano Time
978-0-19-372766-3

Spooky Piano Time
978-0-19-372765-6

'Fresh, original and hugely fun — what more could a piano teacher want?'

Piano Journal

Are you a piano teacher? Would you like to join the OUP piano teachers' mailing list?

Email music.enquiry.uk@oup.com
or phone +44 (0)1865 355067

Piano Time is available from your local music shop, or order from OUP — +44 (0)1536 452630, music.orders.uk@oup.com

www.oup.com/uk/pianotime

MPT12X

Study

♦ Play the left hand first. Did you notice something? Because your fingers already know the scale, you can let your left hand play itself, while you concentrate on your right.

Cornelius Gurlitt (1820–1901)

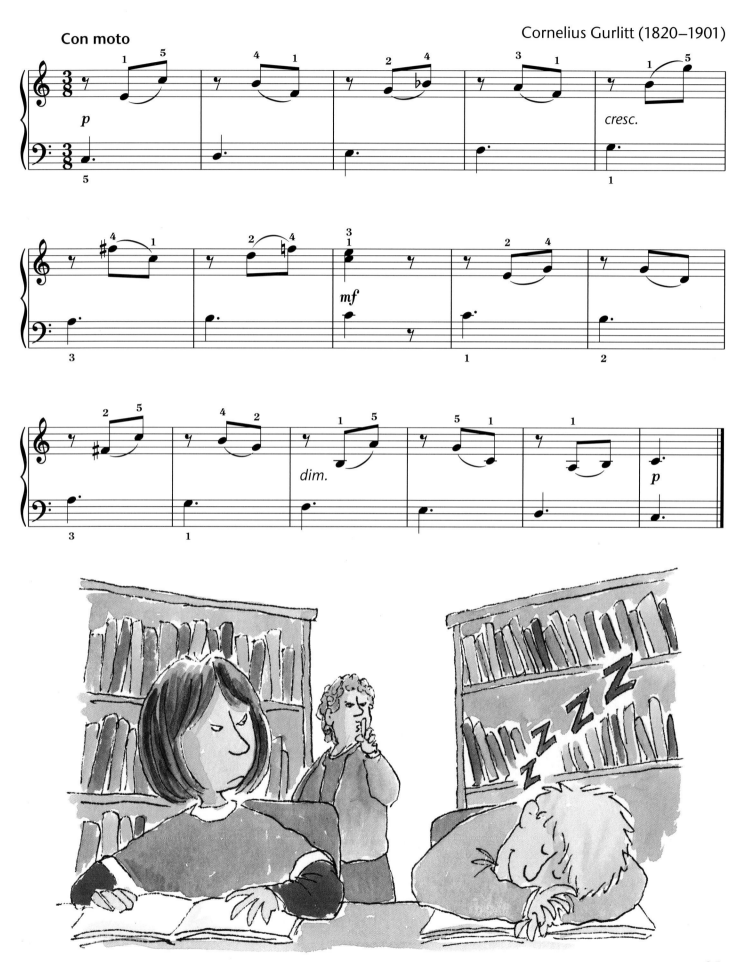

Triplets

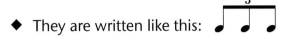

◆ A triplet is a group of three notes that fit into a crotchet ♩

◆ They are written like this:

◆ Because there are three of them, they need to be played a little quicker than quavers to fit them in.

◆ Clap this:

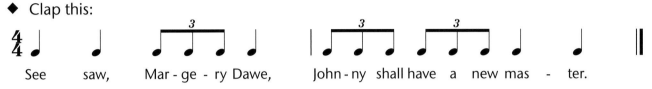

See   saw,   Mar - ge - ry Dawe,   John - ny shall have a new mas - ter.

Twins and triplets

◆ With the same crotchet beat, play 'Twins' and then 'Triplets'. Notice that the triplets need to be played a little faster.

Twins

One twin, two twins, three twins, four;   one twin, two twins, three twins, four.

Triplets

One trip-let, two trip-lets, three trip-lets, four; one trip-let, two trip-lets, three trip-lets, four.

Triplet study

◆ The right-hand triplets must be absolutely even, with no gaps between them. Don't forget that the 5th finger of your left hand holds the first note in each bar for three beats.

Allegretto

Carl Czerny (1791–1857)

The old sailing ship

◆ Which hand do you think is the important one playing the tune and which hand plays the accompaniment? Keep the accompaniment much quieter than the tune part. As usual, practise hands separately before putting them together.

Andante

Pauline Hall

Amazing grace

arr. Pauline Hall

Steadily

Ragamuffin

◆ In this piece your left hand plays all the notes with the stems going down. Make the joins between the hands very neat—there mustn't be any gaps between the 3rd and 4th semiquavers when you change from one hand to the other.

Allegro

Cedric Lamont
arr. Pauline Hall

Jamaica farewell

◆ The time signature of this piece looks a little unusual, but just means that there are eight quavers in the bar. Often these are grouped as 3 + 3 + 2 to give the relaxed rumba rhythm. To start with, and until you feel the swing of the rhythm, count a steady eight in a bar.

Rumba rhythm—with a steady swing

West Indian calypso
arr. Pauline Hall

◆ This piece would sound really good with some extra rhythm. You might try making a shaker out of a plastic bottle with some small stones or rice in it, and getting someone to accompany you.

A restful page

◆ Do you always take notice of rests? If you don't, you may alter a piece of music altogether.

◆ Here are the rests you know:

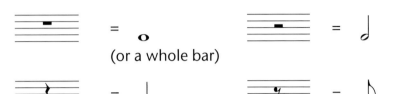

(or a whole bar)

◆ A semiquaver rest looks like this:

◆ A dotted crotchet rest, which is used in $\frac{6}{8}$ time, looks like this: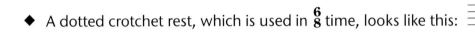

◆ Play the start of this well-known tune:

◆ Here it is again, but with a difference: it is full of rests in unexpected places! Play it again, counting four beats in a bar very carefully.

◆ Now try these two one-handed tunes, counting the rests carefully.

Allegretto

Andante

30

Echoes

◆ Put the left-hand keys down slowly so that they don't sound, and hold them down throughout the piece. Magic! The right-hand notes will make the silent left hand sound. The chords in the right hand are groups of next-door notes.

Allegretto

David Farquhar

Scales hands together, two octaves

◆ Just as with one-octave scales hands together, the secret is to play these scales **very slowly** until they feel secure. **Always** use the right fingering.

The 4th finger bend

◆ This exercise will help the long climb of two octaves. There's a dangerous corner right in the middle of the climb, where you have to swing your 4th finger over your thumbs without bumping. Practise hands separately first and then hands together.

Pauline Hall

◆ The 4th finger bend happens once on the way up (in the left hand) and once on the way down (in the right).

◆ Once this feels comfortable, have a go at the whole scale of C major.

C major

◆ When you can play the scale of C safely with hands together, try the scales of G and D major. Practise the 4th finger bend first and look out for the sharps.

G major

D major

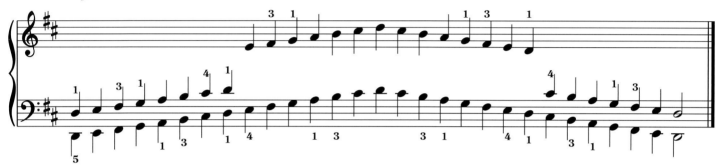

◆ Are your hands still in a good position? Your fingers should be nicely curved and on their tips.

The watermill

Walking tall

With a swing in your step

Alan Bullard

Major and minor

◆ Play this tune:

◆ Now play it again, changing all the Es to E♭s.

◆ Did you notice the difference in sound? You have changed the tune from a **major** key into a **minor** key.

C major   C minor   G major   G minor   F major   F minor

◆ To change a major triad to a minor triad, flatten the middle note.

◆ The D major triad has a sharp in it already. When you flatten a sharpened note, it becomes a natural.

D major   D minor

Spot the chords

◆ Play these chords with your left hand.

Can you hear which ones are **major** and which are **minor**?

Sorrow and joy

◆ This piece is in both D minor and D major.

Alan Bullard

Pictures

- A lot of piano pieces 'paint' a picture or scene or mood. You need to use your imagination and have the picture or idea in your mind as you play.

A cavalry song of the Steppes

- Imagine the Russian horsemen singing this song as they gallop across the plains. '**Con brio**' means 'with spirit', and this piece needs to sound really exciting.

Moon on the distant sea

◆ Can you describe this scene in your playing?

◆ Your right hand plays only two chords:

◆ *una corda* means the left (or soft) pedal. Keep it held down all the way through.

Melodic minor scales

◆ In *Piano Time 2* you learnt to play the **harmonic** minor scale. Here's the A minor harmonic scale:

◆ Remember the big stretch at the top?

◆ The other kind of minor scale is the **melodic** minor scale. Here, instead of sharpening the seventh note only, you sharpen both the **sixth** and **seventh** notes as you go up, and flatten them both as you come down.

◆ The stretchy minor is called the **harmonic** minor.
The non-stretchy minor is called the **melodic** minor.

A minor

Here is the melodic minor scale on A:

Right hand:

Left hand:

D minor

Now try the melodic minor scale on D.

Right hand:

Left hand:

Relative keys

◆ Each minor scale—melodic or harmonic—is the first-cousin of a major key, and uses the same key signature. The minor key is called the 'relative minor' of the major key.

◆ To find the **relative minor**, start on the first note of the major and count down three semitones.

◆ What is the relative minor of G major? . . . .

Minuet

◆ Can you work out what key this piece is in? Key: . . . .

(Two clues: look at the key signature and see if there are any sharps scattered about.)

Andante

Henry Purcell (1659–95)

Plan your own concert

It is a very good thing to get used to playing in front of an audience, even if that audience is only one person! By now you will have learnt lots of pieces which could make up a short concert programme. Here's how to plan it.

◆ Decide on the pieces you like and want to play. Choose pieces that are different from each other—perhaps a short jolly one to start, then a slow quiet one, and then a quick cheerful piece to end with.

◆ Practise these three until they are really secure and there are no mistakes or stumbles. If you can, play them from memory.

◆ It's a good idea to write out a programme. Something like this:

Piano Recital Programme

Given by .... Date..

Title of Piece   Composer

1. .... by ....

2. .... by ....

3. .... by ....

◆ When you've finished, stand up and give a little bow to acknowledge the applause.

◆ You can choose your pieces from earlier in this book or from other *Piano Time* books. There are also some concert pieces on the next few pages.

◆ Enjoy giving your concerts!

Minuet

Grazioso

Wilhelm Friedemann Bach (1710–84)

Goblin dance

Alan Bullard

Not too fast and a bit sinister: staccato throughout

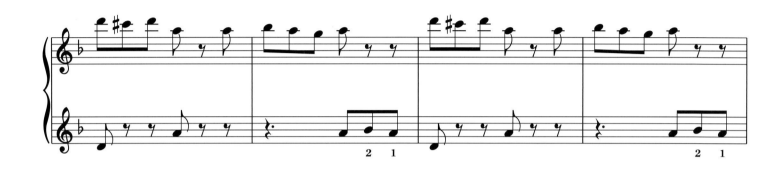

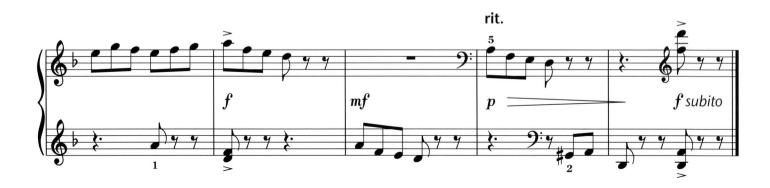

Rippling stream

Allegretto grazioso

Pauline Hall

Moderato

◆ Your left hand is the accompanist in this piece, so be very careful not to let it get loud and heavy, especially where it has repeated chords.

attrib. D. G. Türk (1756–1813)
ed. Pauline Hall

Oxford rag

With intelligence, and not too fast

Alan Bullard

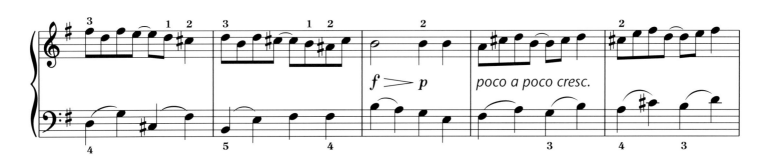

Musical terms

◆ By now you know lots of the Italian terms used to give directions about how to play—what speed, how loud or soft, how to play the notes, and so on. There are a few new ones added here that it's worth getting to know.

Speeds and style

Allargando	broadening the speed (slowing up a little)
Allegretto	a little slower than **Allegro**
Allegro	brisk and lively
Andante	at a walking pace
Cantabile	with a singing tone
Con brio	with spirit, with energy
Con moto	with movement
Espressivo	expressively
Grazioso	gracefully
Leggiero	lightly
Maestoso	majestically
Marcato	accented
A tempo	in time; back to the original speed (after a **ritenuto**)
Tranquillo	calmly

Loud or soft

pp	***p***	***mp***	***mf***	***f***	***ff***
very soft	soft	moderately soft	moderately loud	loud	very loud

crescendo = getting louder
diminuendo = getting quieter

Where to go

‖: :‖	repeat signs
1.	first time bar
2.	second time bar
D.C. (*Da Capo*)	go back to the beginning
Fine	the end
8va‐ ‐ ‐ ‐ ‐ ¬	play the notes an octave higher
8va bassa	play the notes an octave lower

One or two extras!

e sim.	and similarly
poco	a little
sempre	always
subito	suddenly
una corda	use the left (or soft) pedal